AF413636

Where Did You Get the Color of Your Eyes?

Hereditary Patterns Science Book for Kids

Children's Biology Books

BABY PROFESSOR

EDUCATION KIDS

Speedy Publishing LLC

40 E. Main St. #1156

Newark, DE 19711

www.speedypublishing.com

Copyright 2017

You inherit the information for how your body looks, works, and grows from your parents. The information is in the 23 chromosome pairs in your cells, and each parent gives you half of each chromosome pair.

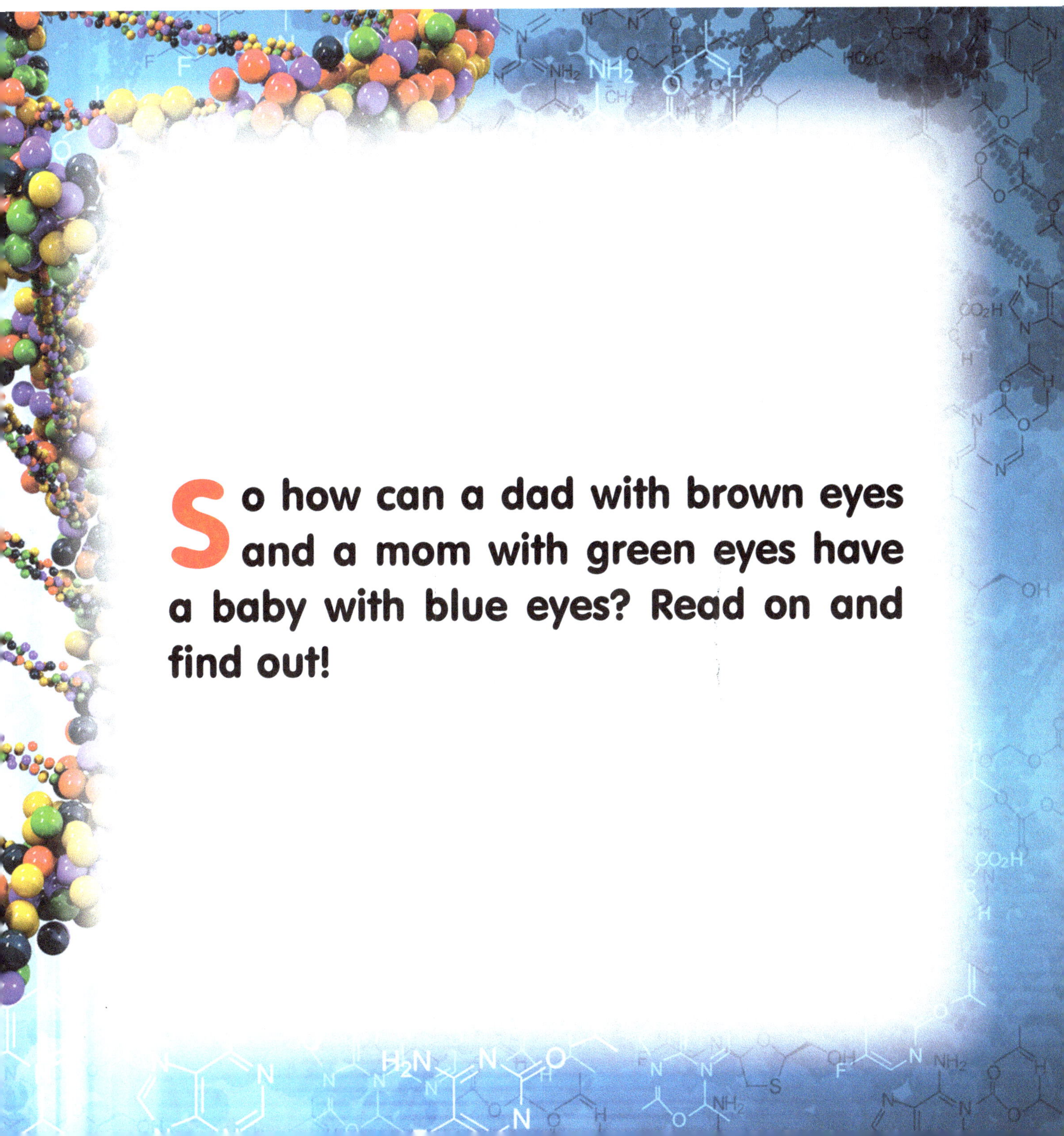

So how can a dad with brown eyes and a mom with green eyes have a baby with blue eyes? Read on and find out!

DOMINANT AND RECESSIVE

Each chromosome in your body has many genes, and those genes carry instructions: make this person taller or shorter! Give this person more curly hair! They also give the instructions that tell your body to build your rib cage and your organs, to give you the right number of fingers and toes, and organize all the other features of your wonderful body.

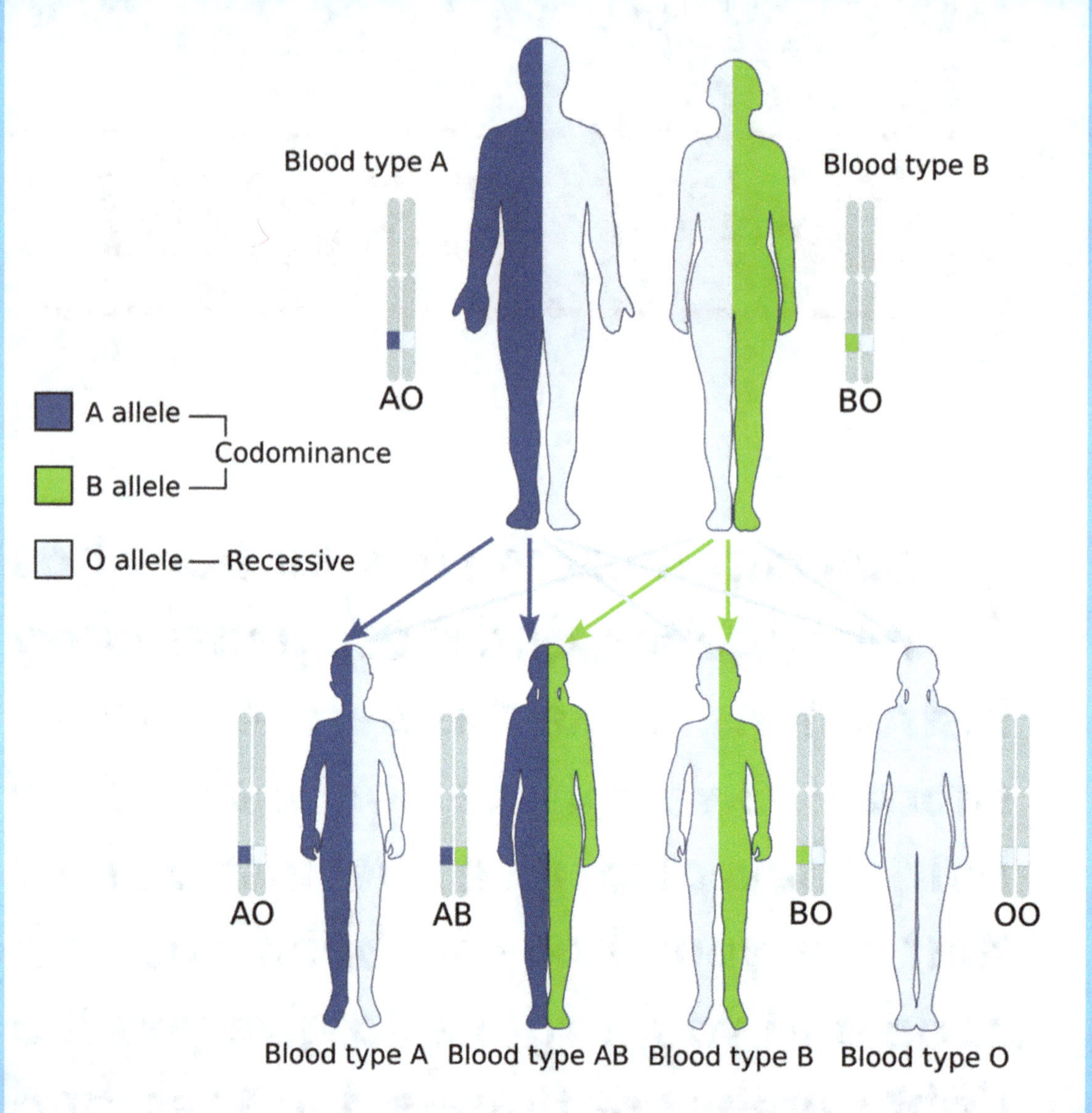

Medelian Traits

Since you get half of the instructions from your father (who might have curly hair) and your mother (who might have straight hair), a lot of the time the instructions don't match each other. Then the gene that is stronger (dominant) tends to deliver its instructions more often than the gene that's weaker (recessive).

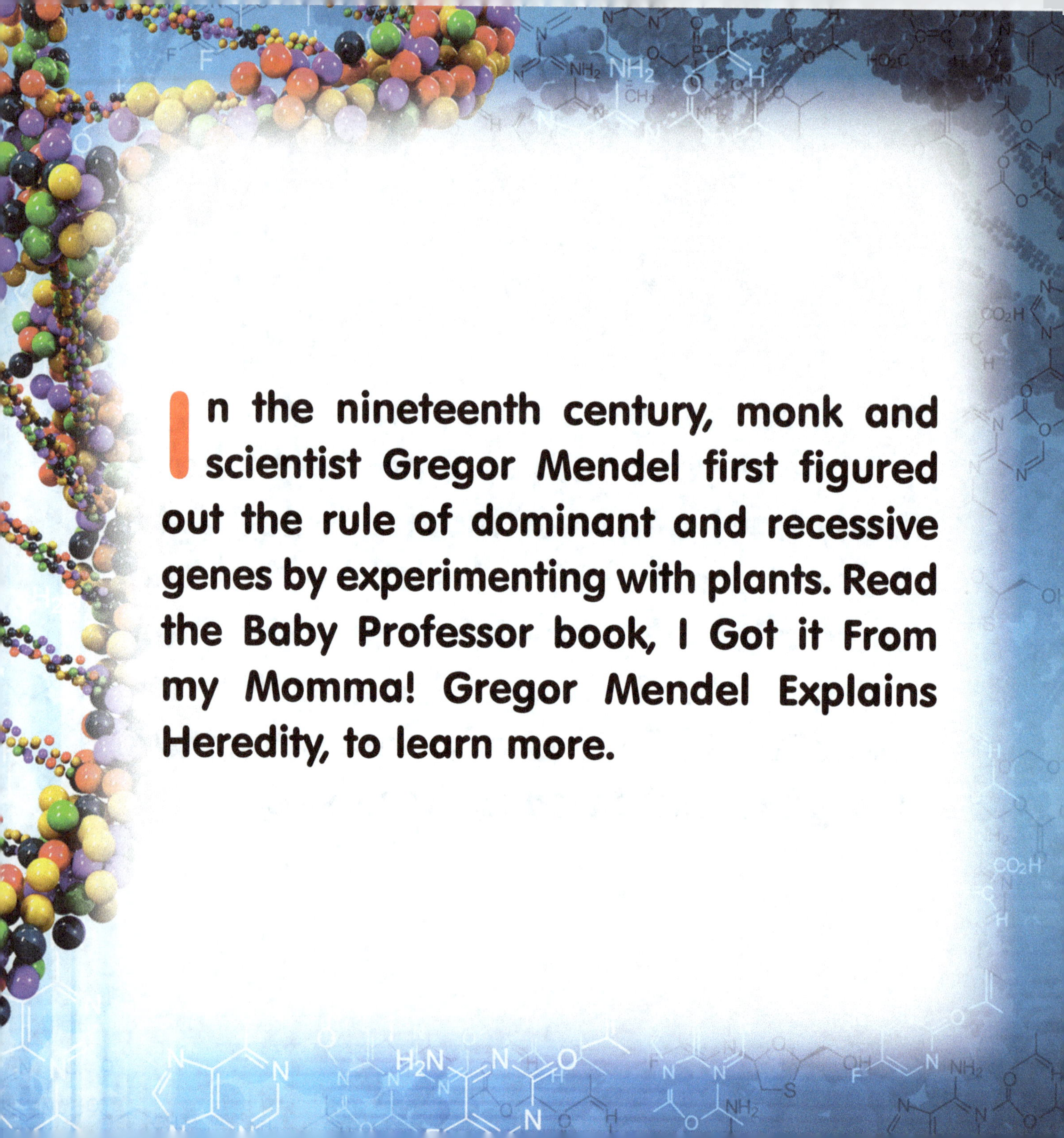

In the nineteenth century, monk and scientist Gregor Mendel first figured out the rule of dominant and recessive genes by experimenting with plants. Read the Baby Professor book, I Got it From my Momma! Gregor Mendel Explains Heredity, to learn more.

Gregor Mendel

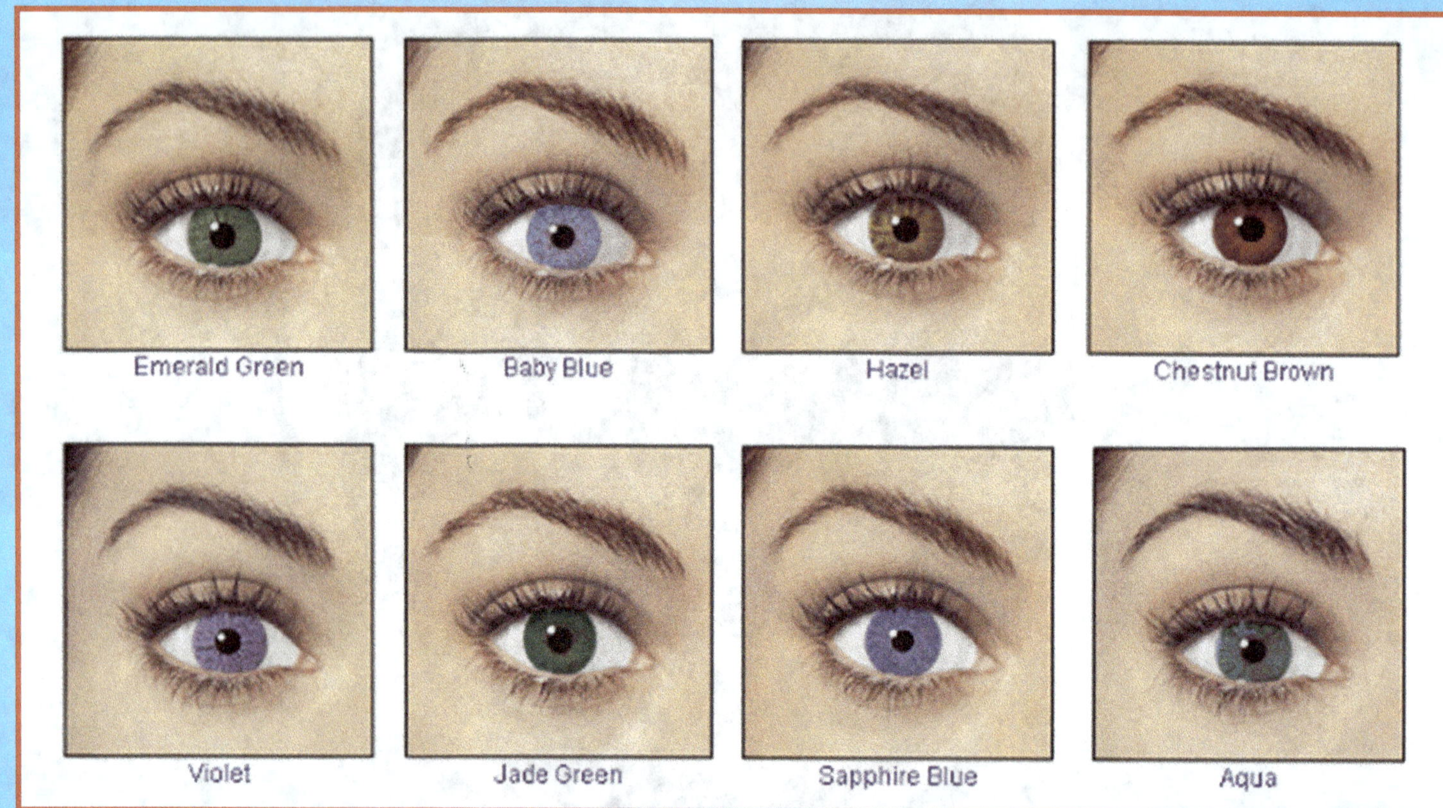

Eye Color Chart

THE SIMPLE MODEL

For eye color, we had a simple model: we thought there were two genes that controlled eye color. One gave instruction for making the eyes brown (B) or blue (b), and the other for making the eyes green (G) or blue (b).

Do they have the same eye color?

However, the more we learn, the more we understand that the whole process of inheriting traits is more complicated than we first thought. The simple model above did not cover situations like how parents who both have blue eyes can have a child with brown eyes.

PIGMENT AND DARKNESS

Your eye color is a combination of what happens in two layers in the iris, the colored area around the pupil of your eye. One layer gets the basic color: blue. The other layer, called the stroma, gets melanin, a pigment, in varying amounts depending on the instructions in your genes. Lots of melanin in the stroma gives you brown eyes. Less melanin gives you green eyes. And if you have little or no melanin in the stroma, you have blue eyes.

A baby's eyes are blue at birth, no matter what color they become later, because neither the pigment nor the melanin have become active until the eyes start reacting to light. It may take until age three for the baby's eyes to start showing the color they will have for the rest of the person's life.

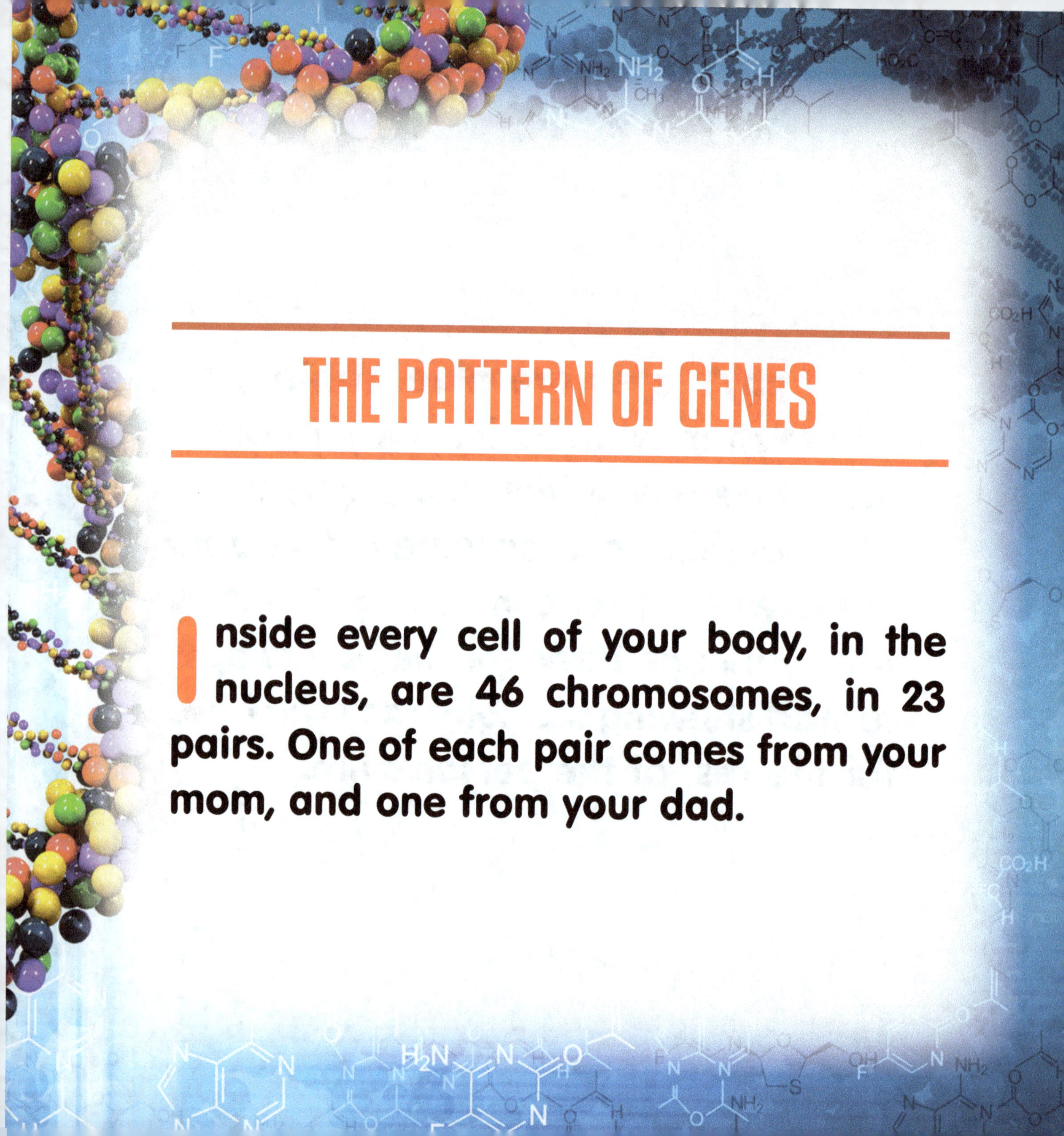

THE PATTERN OF GENES

Inside every cell of your body, in the nucleus, are 46 chromosomes, in 23 pairs. One of each pair comes from your mom, and one from your dad.

DNA

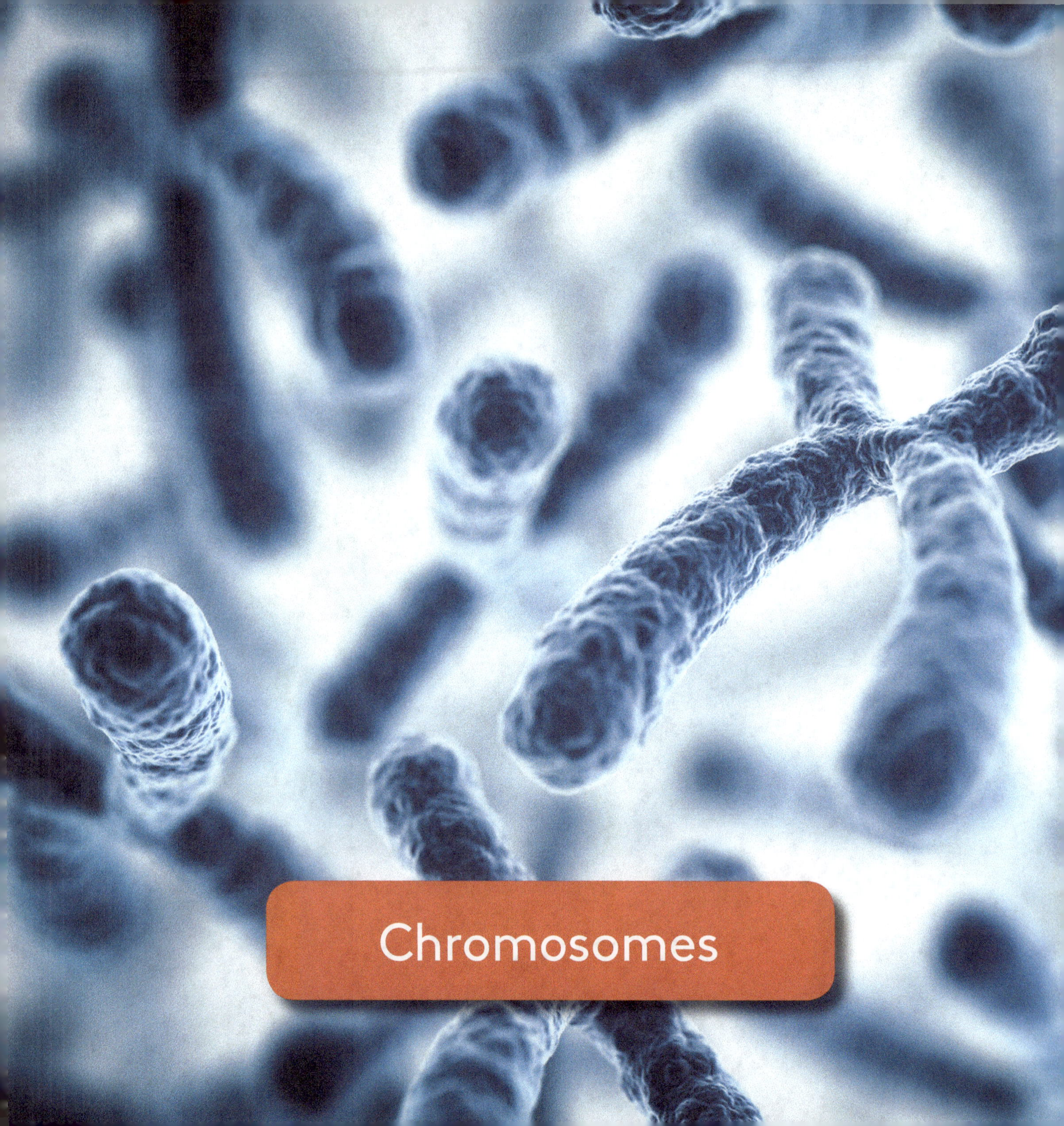

Chromosomes

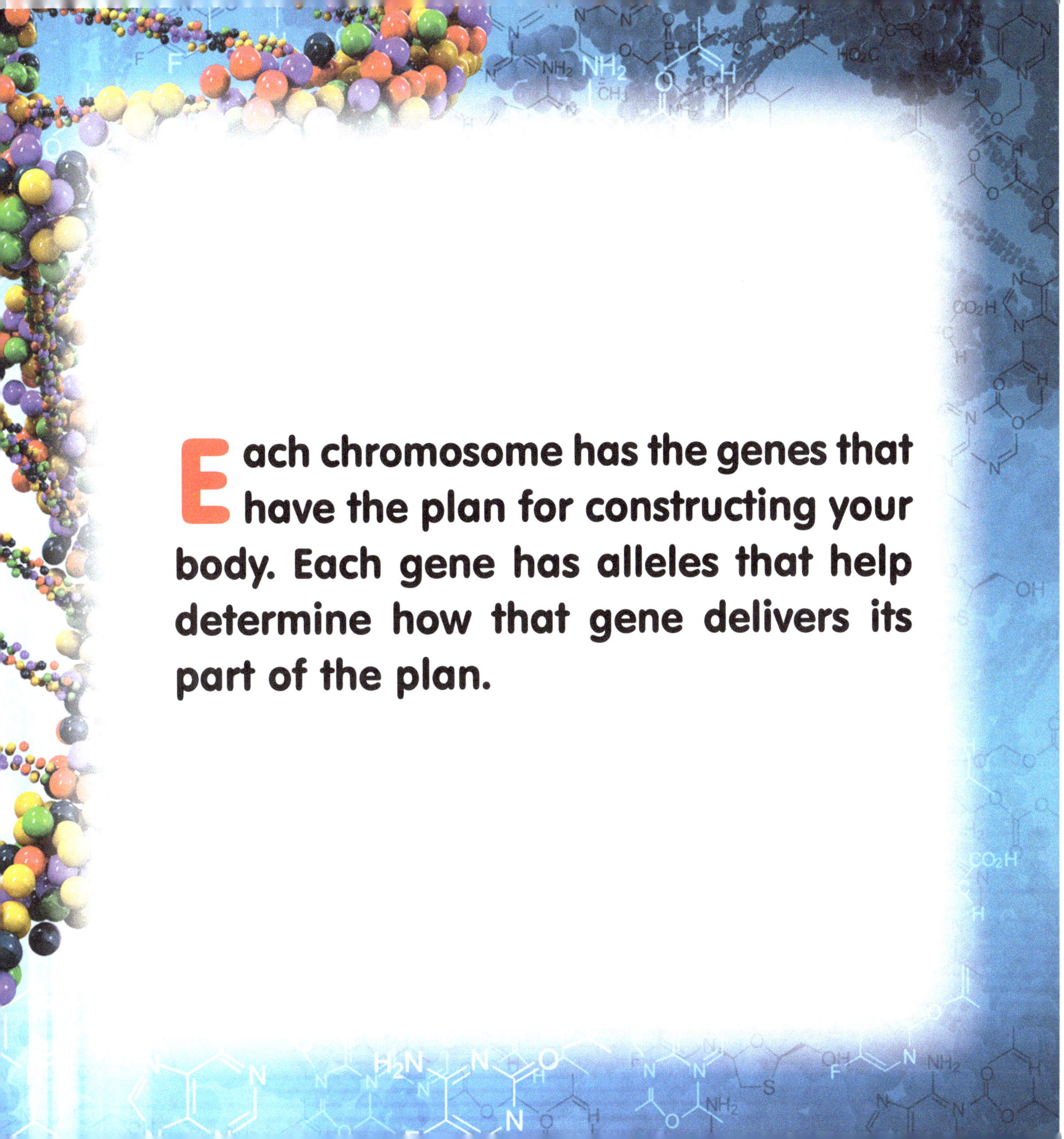

Each chromosome has the genes that have the plan for constructing your body. Each gene has alleles that help determine how that gene delivers its part of the plan.

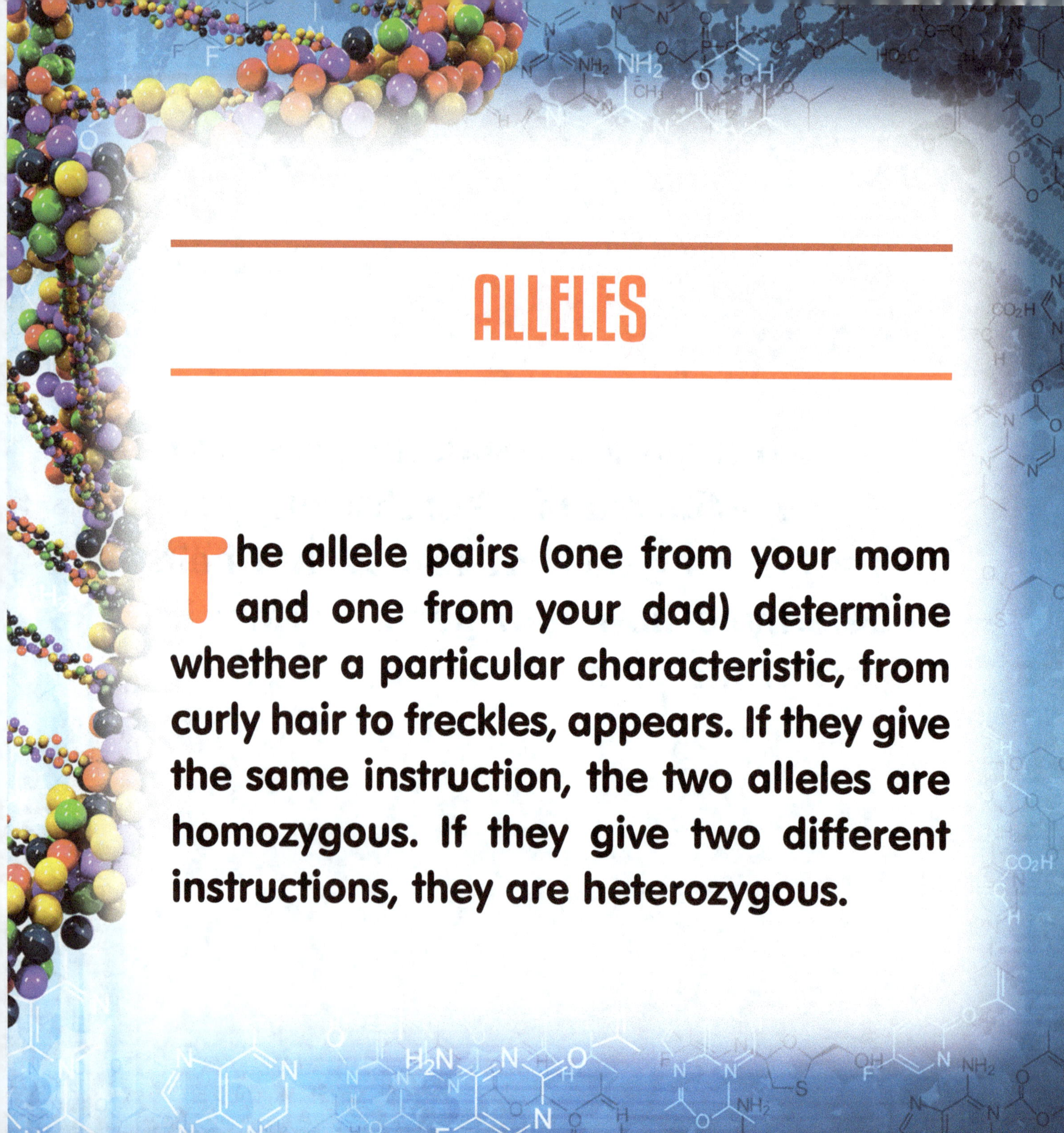

ALLELES

The allele pairs (one from your mom and one from your dad) determine whether a particular characteristic, from curly hair to freckles, appears. If they give the same instruction, the two alleles are homozygous. If they give two different instructions, they are heterozygous.

If you have a homozygous allele pair, no problem! It just sends its instruction on to the body.

Eye color
Blood type
Hair color
Growth

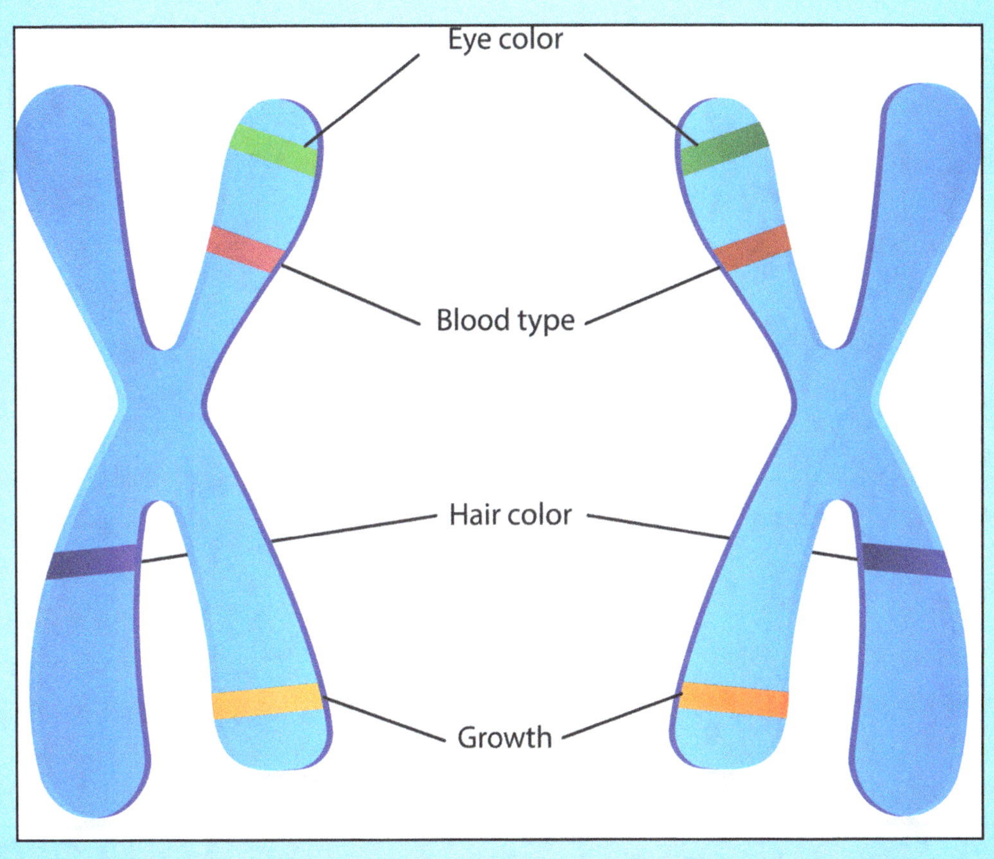

Alleles

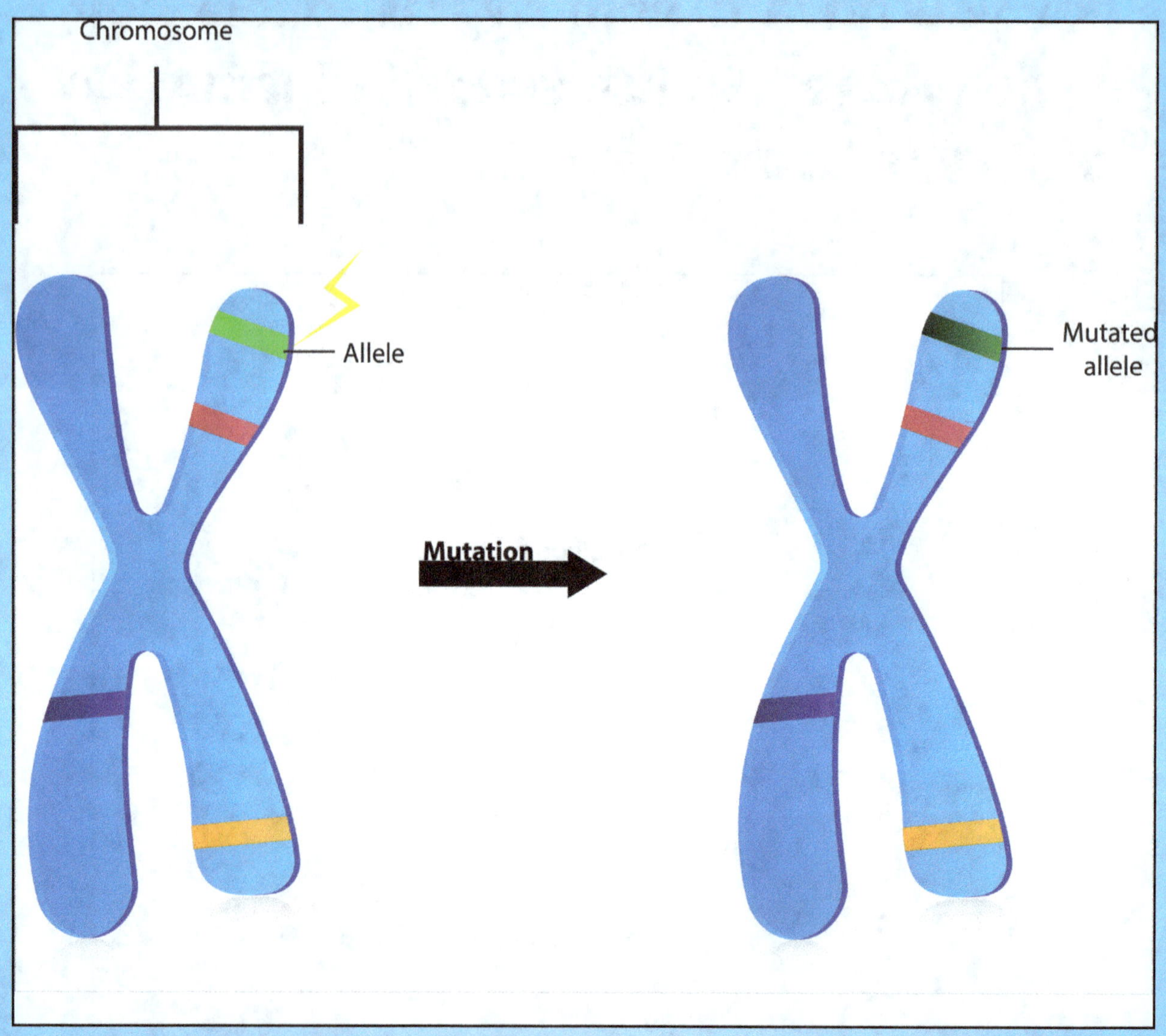

Mutation of a chromosome

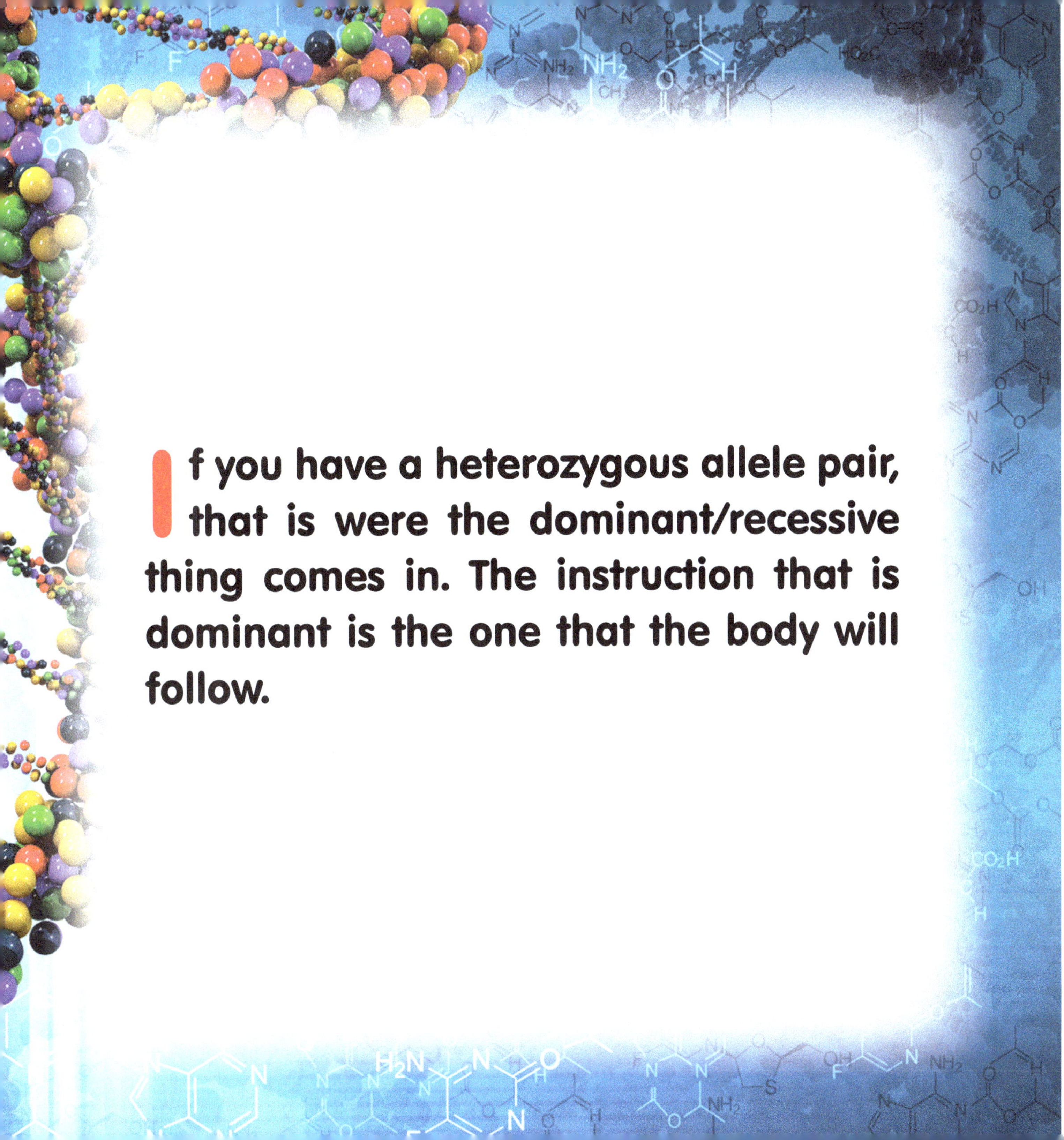

If you have a heterozygous allele pair, that is were the dominant/recessive thing comes in. The instruction that is dominant is the one that the body will follow.

ALLELES FOR EYE COLOR

Here's where it gets interesting. Not only are there as many as 16 different genes that play a part in determining eye color, instead of the two that we originally thought we had to worry about, there are not two, but three basic choices.

PARENTS
BABY'S EYE COLOR

75%
18,75%
6,25%

50%
37,5%
12,5%

50%
50%
0%

75%
25%
<1%

 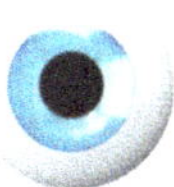   

50%
50%
0%

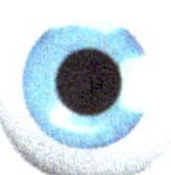  

99%
1%
0%

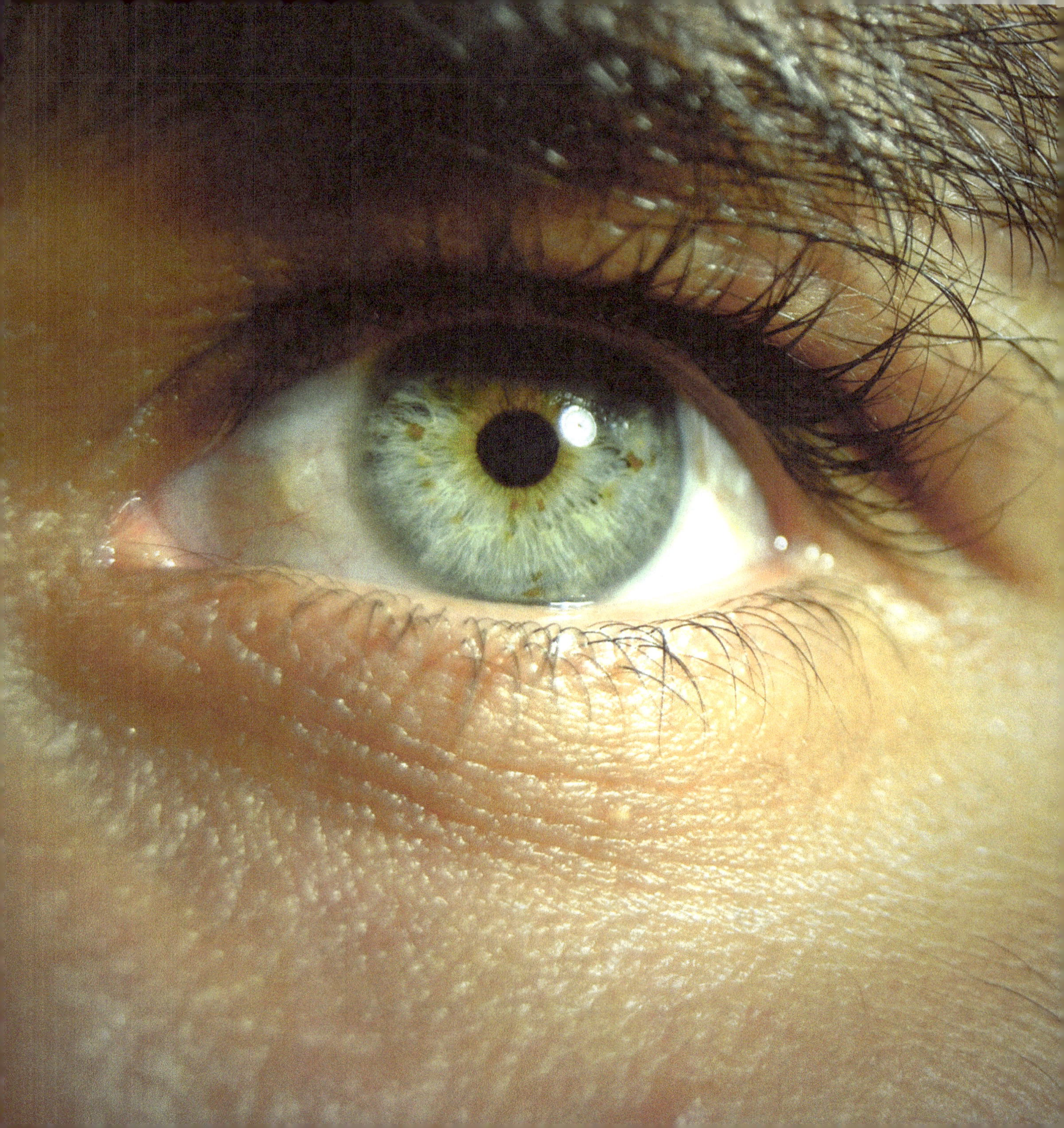

The alleles for eye color can be for blue, green, or brown. If the instruction is for green eyes, it is dominant over an instruction for blue eyes. An instruction for brown eyes is dominant over both other colors. If you get a brown instruction (dominant) and a blue instruction, you will end up with brown eyes. If you have blue eyes, then you got a blue allele instruction from both your mother and your father.

However, because there are all those genes at play, other combinations of allele instructions can affect how green, blue, or brown your eyes appear, or even whether they sometimes seem more green and sometimes more brown. You can't just look at the parents' eyes and know for absolute, certain, what color the eyes of the child will be.

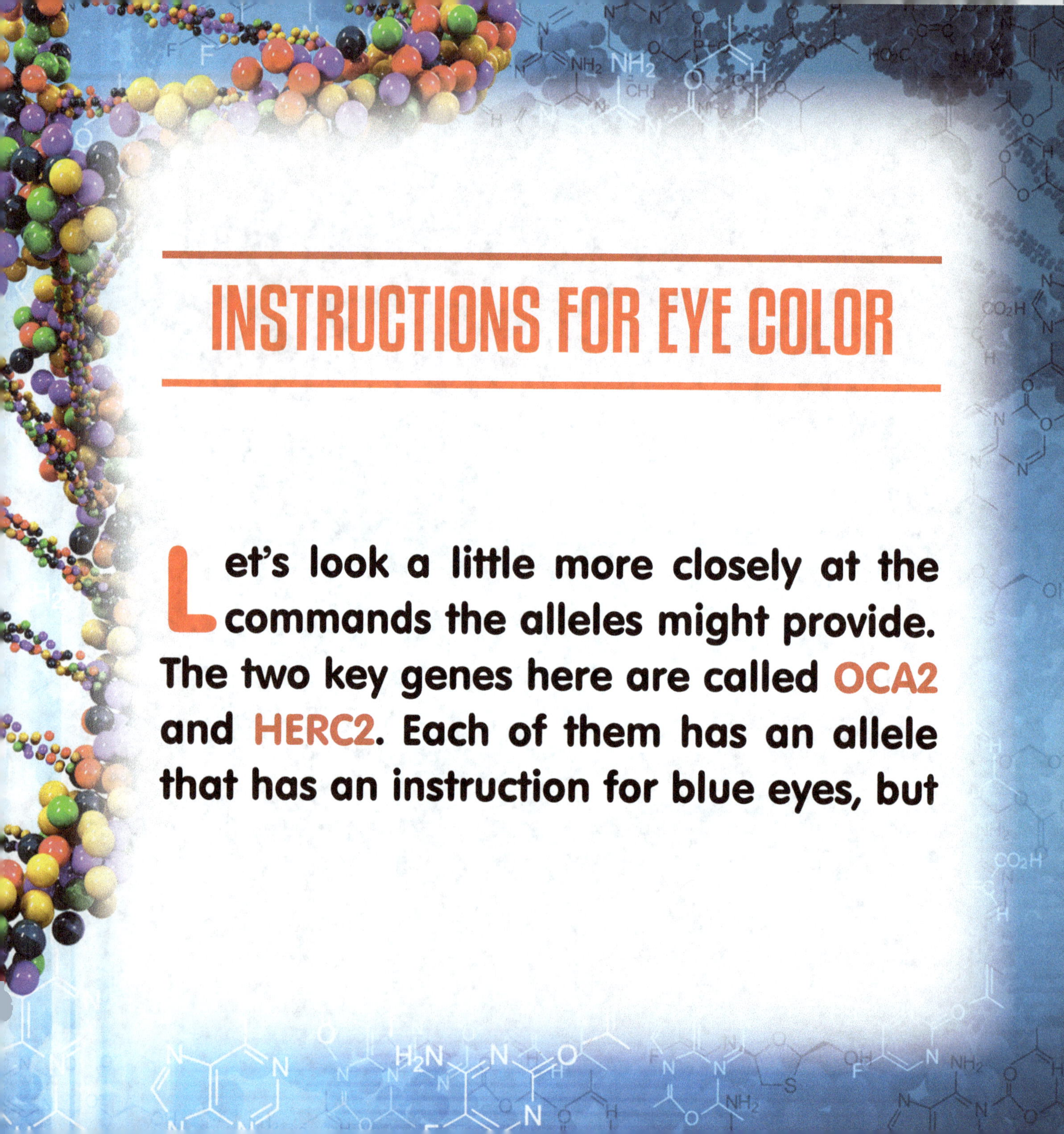

INSTRUCTIONS FOR EYE COLOR

Let's look a little more closely at the commands the alleles might provide. The two key genes here are called OCA2 and HERC2. Each of them has an allele that has an instruction for blue eyes, but you need the blue-eye instruction from each gene, not just from one, for the body to accept the instruction.

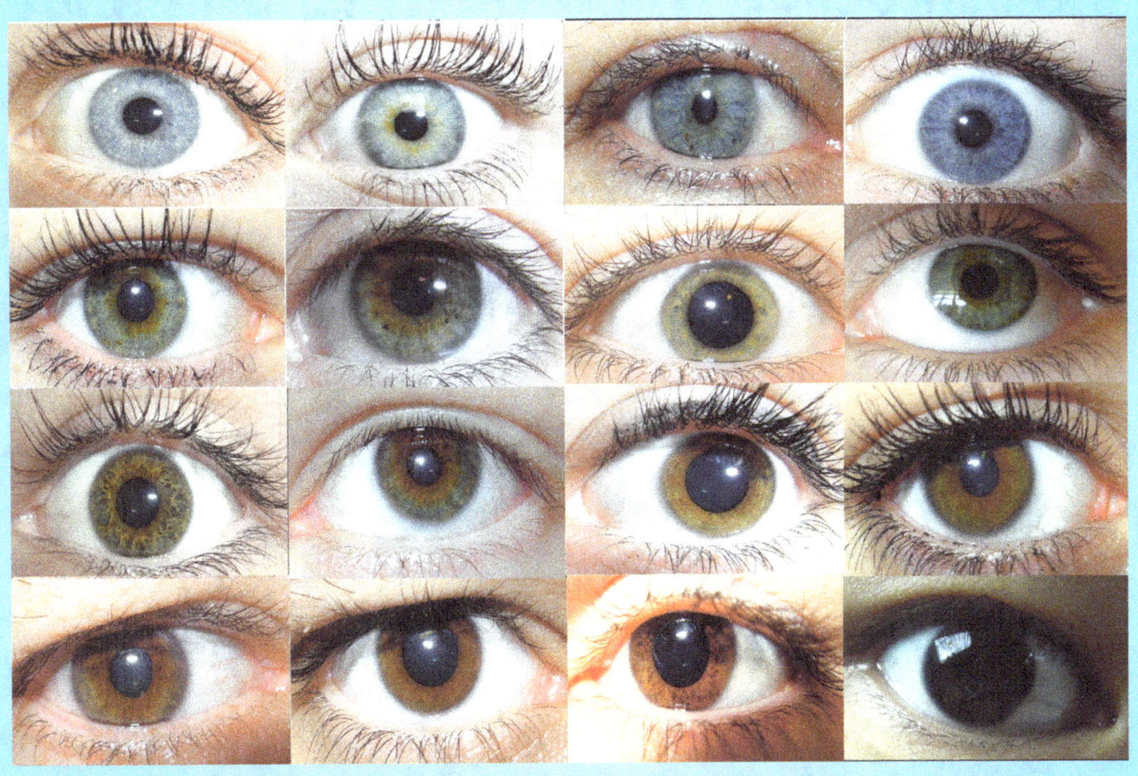

or simplicity, let's say OCA2 provides either the instruction O (brown eyes) or o (blue eyes). And HERC2 provides either the instruction H (brown eyes) or h (blue

eyes). You can end up with any of these combinations of instructions, leading to the result indicated:

OO HH =   brown eyes
OO Hh =   brown eyes
OO hh =   blue eyes
Oo HH =   brown eyes
Oo Hh =   brown eyes
Oo hh =   blue eyes
oo HH =   blue eyes
oo Hh =   blue eyes
oo hh =   blue eyes

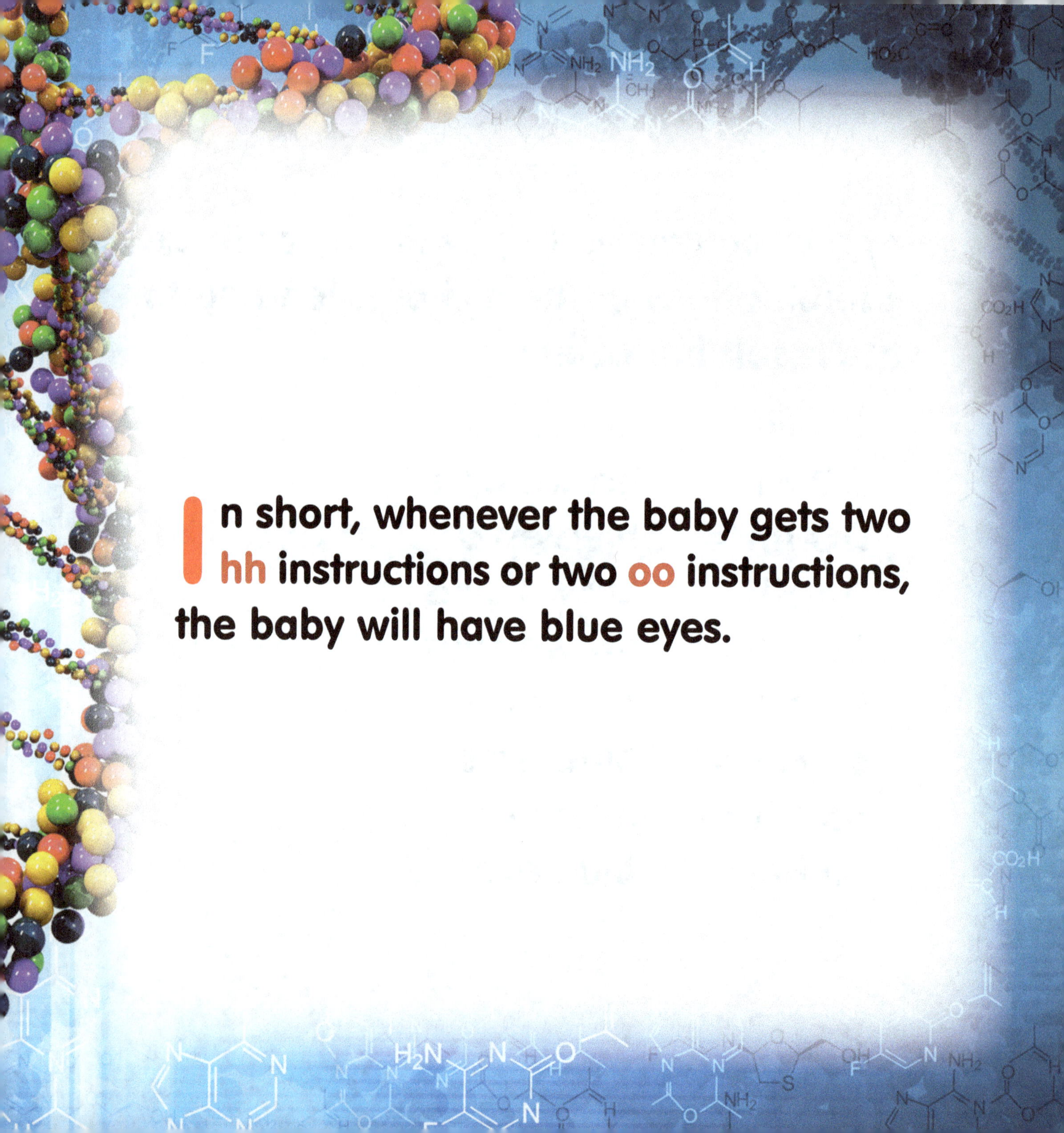

In short, whenever the baby gets two hh instructions or two oo instructions, the baby will have blue eyes.

THE THREE-COLOR MIX

Here's another example, which recognizes that there are instructions for brown, blue and green. One gene directs B (brown) or b (blue). The other gene directs G (green) or b (blue). Remember that brown is dominant over the other two colors and green is dominant over blue.

Here you can get any of these instructions and results:

BB bb =	brown eyes
BB Gb =	brown eyes
BB GG =	brown eyes (brown is dominant over green)
Bb bb =	brown eyes
Bb Gb =	brown eyes
Bb GG =	brown eyes (brown is still dominant!)
bb GG =	green eyes
bb Gb =	green eyes
bb bb =	blue eyes

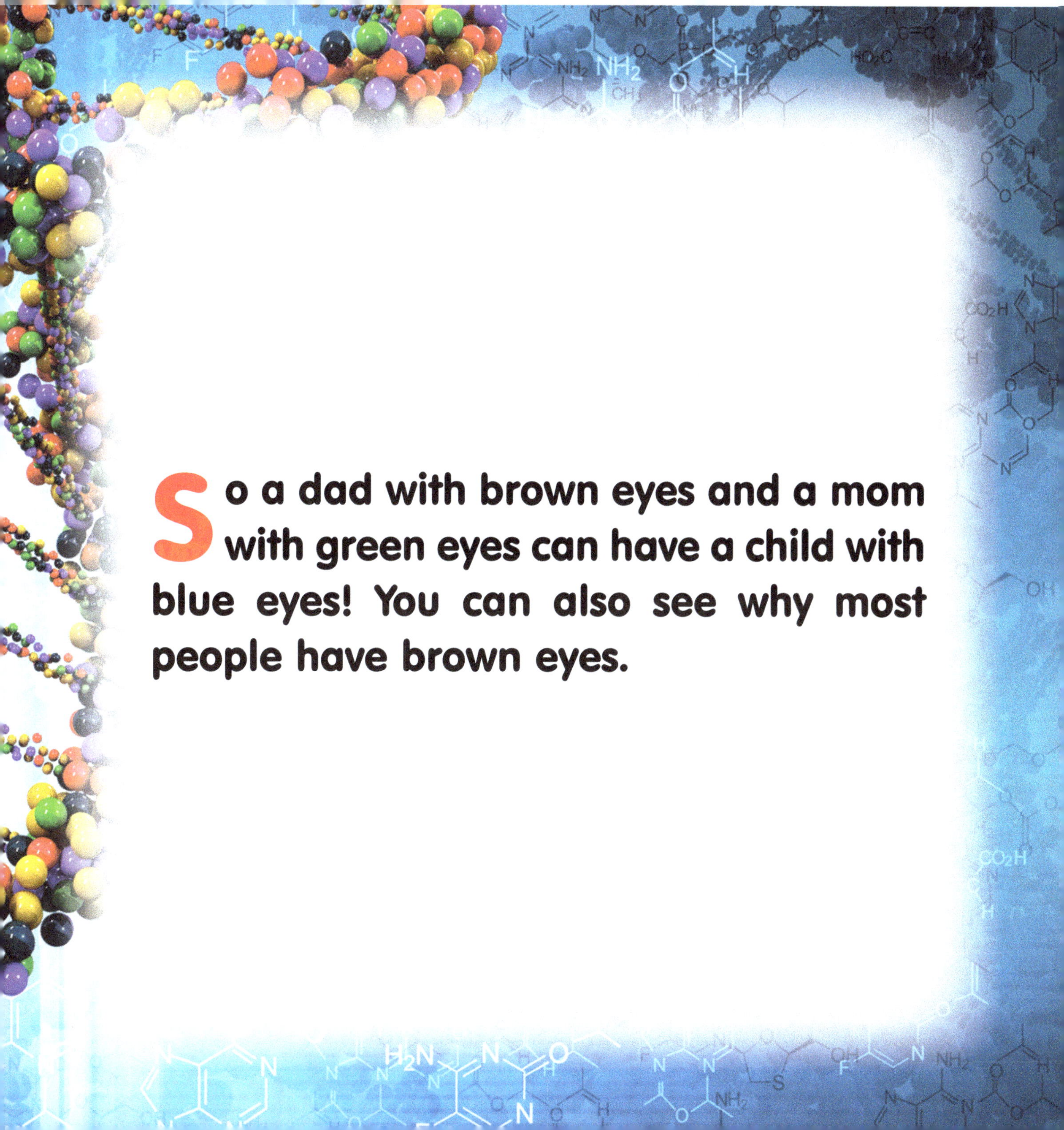

So a dad with brown eyes and a mom with green eyes can have a child with blue eyes! You can also see why most people have brown eyes.

DIFFERENT-COLORED EYES

You sometimes meet people who have eyes of two different colors. This isn't really related to genetics, but to a rare and harmless condition called heterochromia, which causes the irises of your two eyes to develop a little differently from each other.

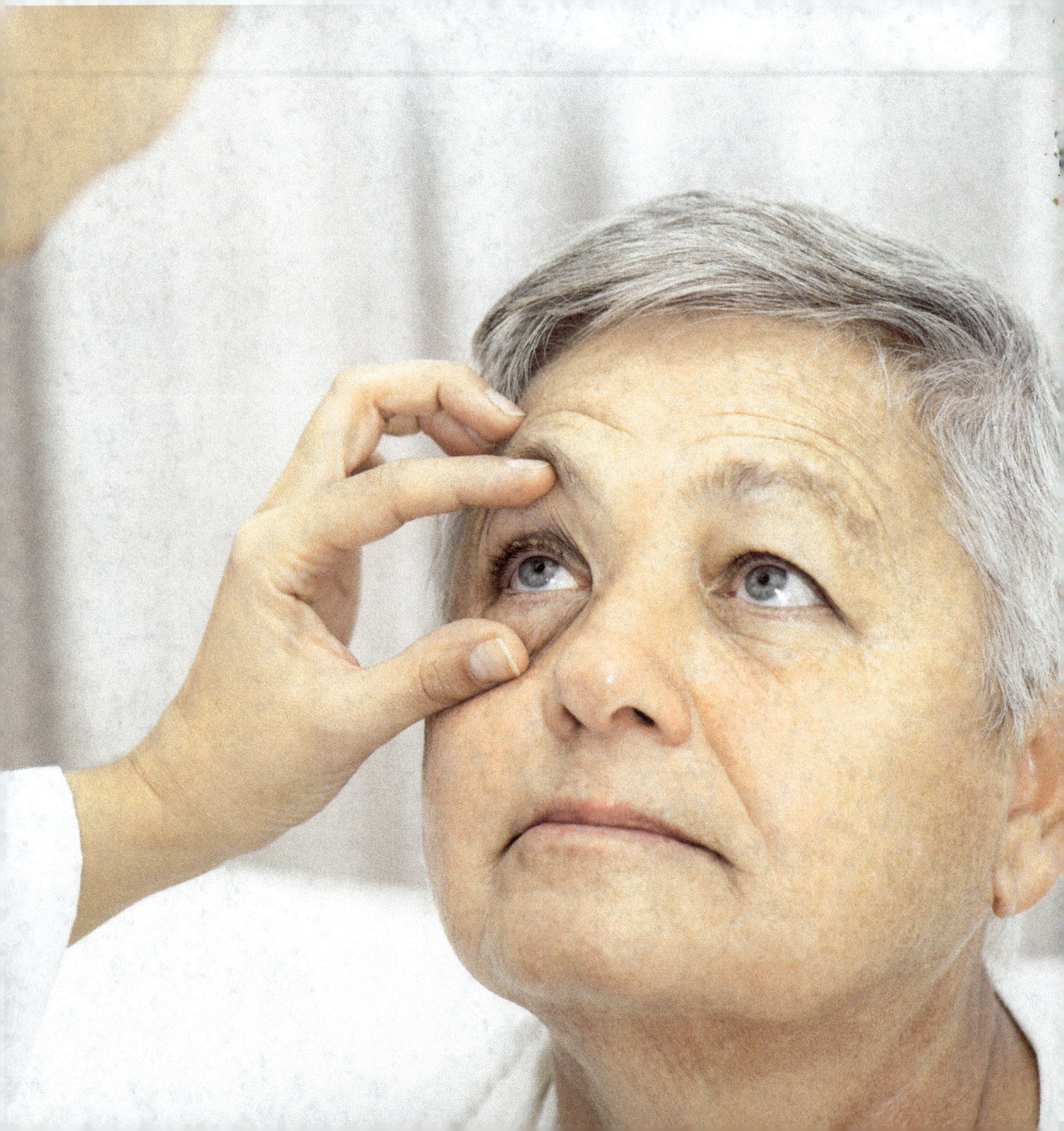

EYE COLORS AND YOUR HEALTH

No matter how you got the color of your eyes, you can learn a bit about your health from that color. Here are some examples:

Blue eyes are more sensitive to light because there is less melanin in the stroma to protect the eyes against the light.

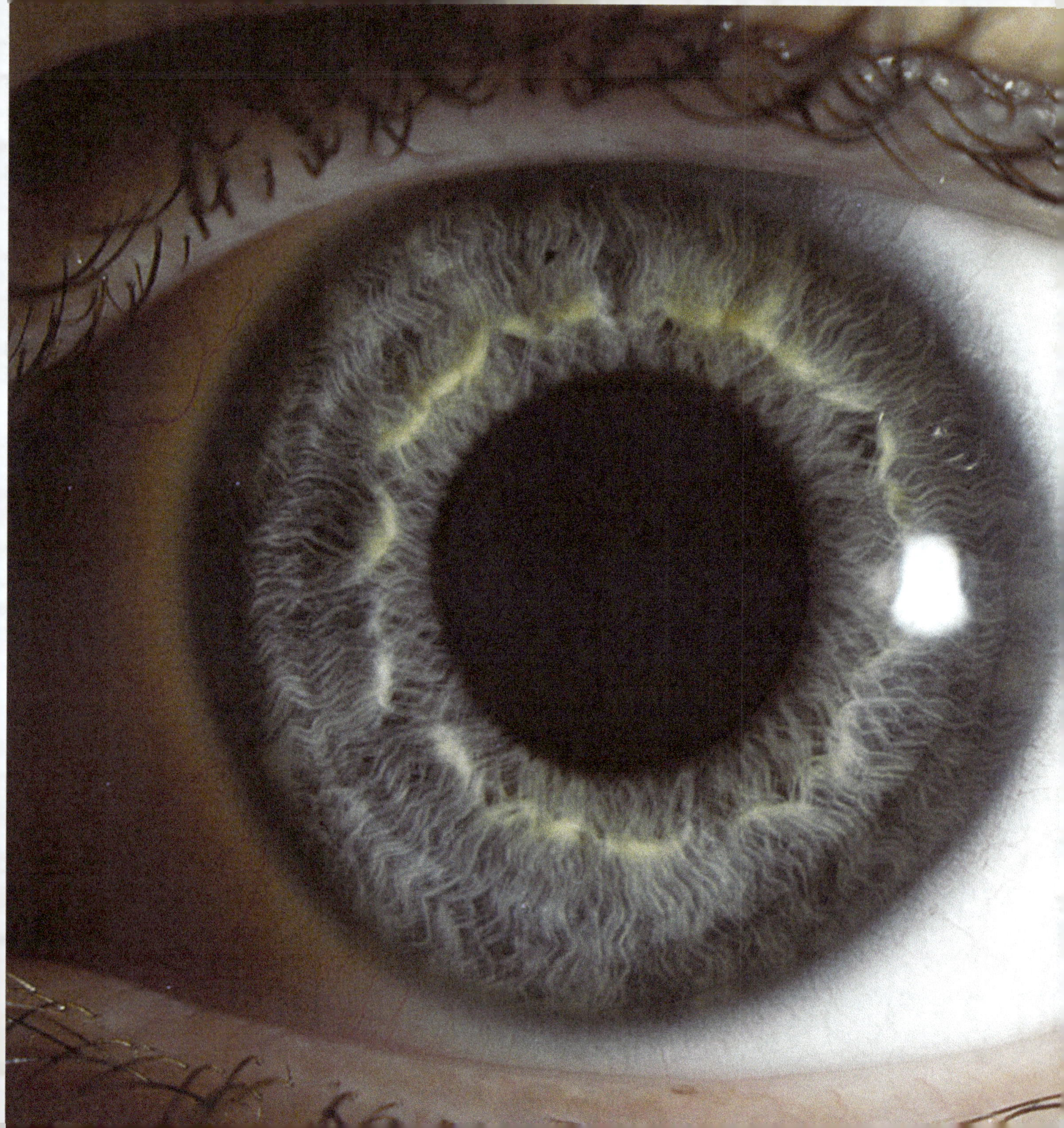

People with gray, green, or blue eyes are more likely to get a rare form of cancer of the eye. As these people also tend to have fair skin, they are more likely to get skin cancer. Just as you use sunblock on your skin, you should wear sunglasses or a cap with a brim to help protect your eyes.

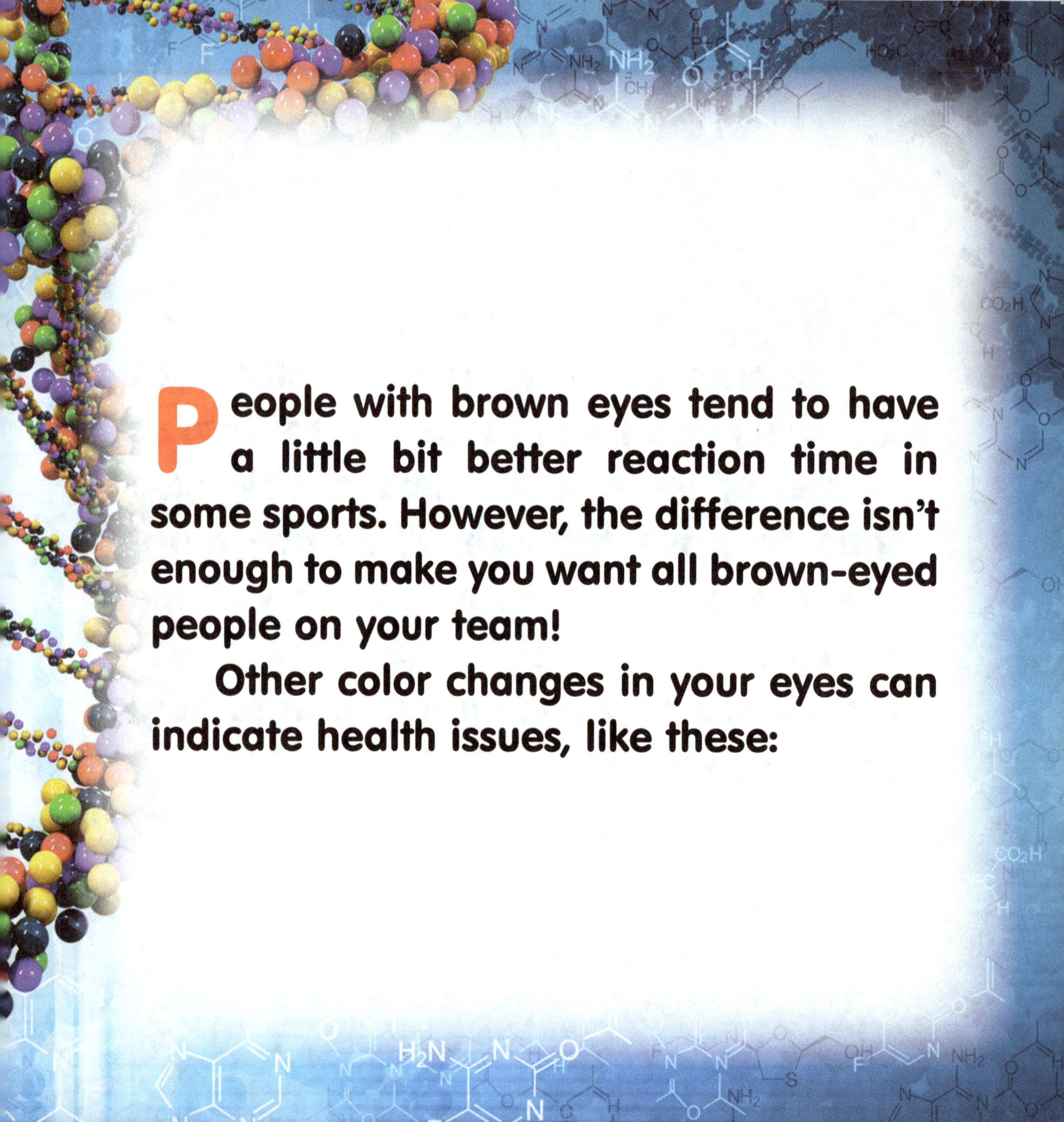

People with brown eyes tend to have a little bit better reaction time in some sports. However, the difference isn't enough to make you want all brown-eyed people on your team!

Other color changes in your eyes can indicate health issues, like these:

If the whites of your eyes are red, that can be caused by allergies, and infection or dryness. Eye drops can help with dryness, but if the redness continues you should see a doctor. If the whites of your eyes are yellowish, that may be jaundice, an indication that something is wrong with your liver. If this is a new thing, you should definitely tell a doctor about it.

A white ring around the cornea, the lens of the eye, can be caused by an increase of cholesterol in the body. This is another thing to mention to the doctor as soon as you notice it.

If there is fogginess over the pupils of your eyes, that could be a sign that you are developing cataracts. The doctor can confirm this or tell you it's nothing to worry about.

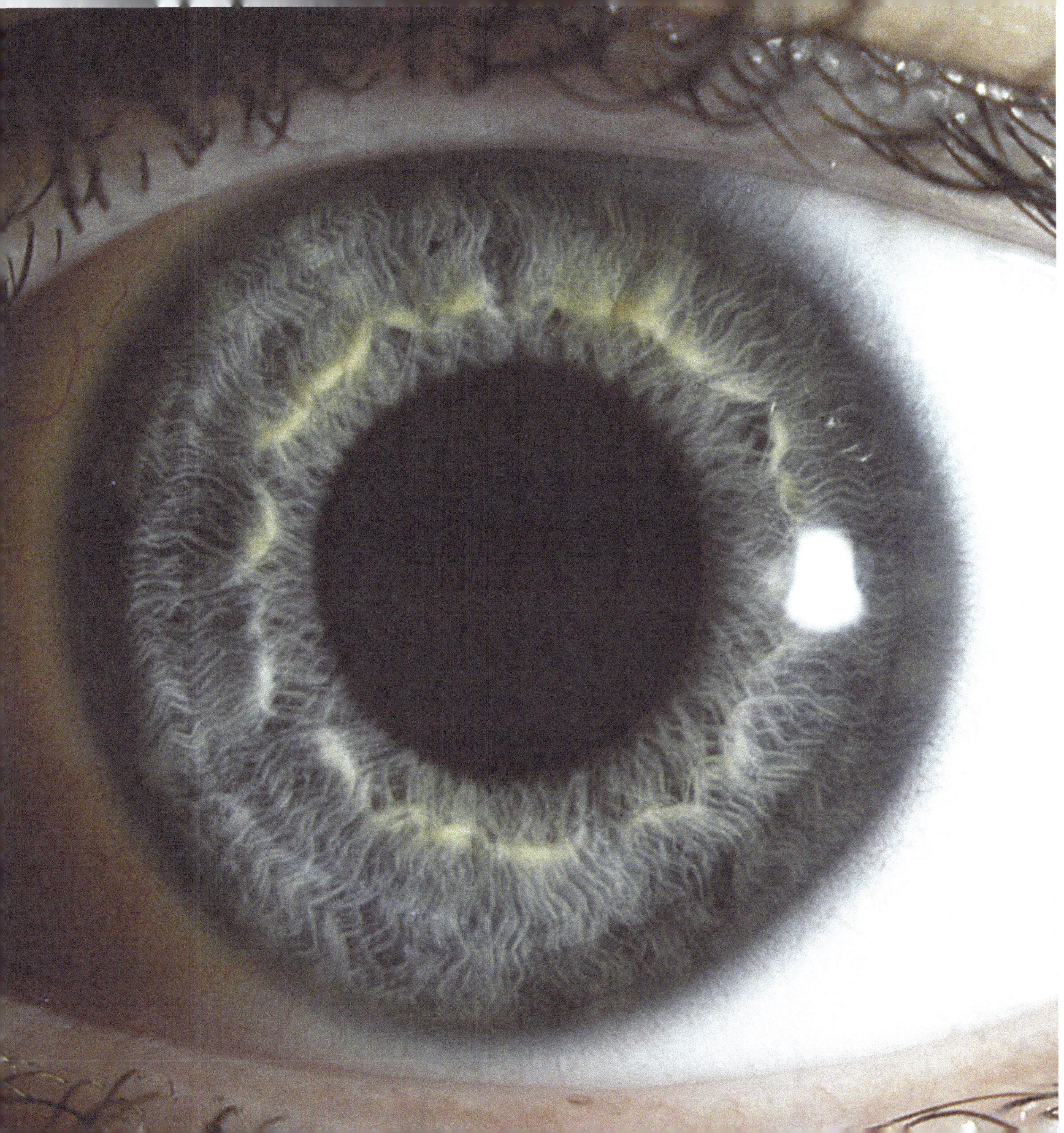

YOUR SURPRISING BODY

There is a lot more to learn about your body—how it works, and what happens when it is not working well. Read other Baby Professor books, like Will this Pill Make Me Better?, *Top 50 Quick Facts about the Human Body*, and *I Got It from My Momma! Gregor Mendel Explains Heredity*, to learn even more!